HOW TO WRITE A BOOK—PERIOD!

No Glitz, No Glam;
Just How To Write a Book

TIMOTHY O. BOND

www.TrueVinePublishing.org

How To Write A Book—Period!
Timothy O. Bond

Published by True Vine Publishing Co.
810 Dominican Dr.
Nashville, TN 37228
www.TrueVinePublishing.org

ISBN: 978-1-962783-64-4

To you,
The brave spirit who has taken the first step to writing
your name in the annals of American literary history.
May this book guide, inspire, motivate, and empower
you to change the world with your book.

TABLE OF CONTENTS

INTRODUCTION

"How do you write a book?"

This is a question I hear almost every day, and it's the driving force behind this book. There is truly only one way to write a book: write it. However, I understand that most people believe the process is more complicated than that. So, it's my goal to address this question in the simplest way possible.

First, let me explain that every writer has their own process. Writing a book is not brain surgery. You can approach it with precision—pre-planning every paragraph, dotting every "i" and crossing every "t" before you even begin writing. Or, you can dive in like a kid at a food fight, slinging messy words on clean white pages until you have piles of raw content. Both methods work. One path may take less time—but it may not be the one you expect.

In my experience, writers who obsess over perfection—making sure every letter is flawless and being afraid to make mistakes—are often the ones who take the longest to finish their book. Meanwhile, the writer who embraces imperfection has written their book, made corrections, and is already working on their next one.

This book is not meant to be an exhaustive manual on the writing process. Rather, its purpose is to help you get out of your own way and just start putting words on paper, for heaven's sake. I'm going to share some strategies on how to stop over-thinking, break through preconceived notions about writing, and hopefully guide you step by step through your first draft.

You'll notice a line of small print at the bottom of every page. If you look closely, you'll see the phrase: "If you don't have the skill or desire, there are others who can do it for you." I'm adding this to every page because it's important. If you don't have the skill or desire, there are others who can help you. Don't get discouraged, and don't feel intimidated if you come across a chapter that seems beyond your current abilities. It's not your job to master every aspect of writing. Your job is to execute what you can and let the professionals handle the rest. Don't psych yourself out. Remember: if you don't have the skill or desire, there are others who can do it for you.

Let's get started!

GETTING STARTED

WRITING CHECKLIST

Writing a book isn't just about having a great idea—it's about having the right tools, discipline, and process to get your words on paper. Below is a fundamental checklist to help you successfully complete your manuscript.

- ❑ Desktop or laptop computer
- ❑ Google docs account
- ❑ Pens and/or pencils
- ❑ Journal
- ❑ Digital audio recorder
- ❑ A preferred writing spot
- ❑ A preferred writing time
- ❑ A trusted beta reader
- ❑ An editor and proofreader

A DESKTOP OR LAPTOP COMPUTER

Even if you love writing by hand, at some point, your manuscript needs to be in digital format. A computer makes it easier to edit, format, and share your work with beta readers, editors, and proofreaders. If typing isn't your strength, you can always hire someone to transcribe your handwritten notes.

GOOGLE DOCS (or Another Cloud-Based Writing Tool)

If you have a Gmail account, you automatically have

access to Google Docs. This tool gives you one of the easiest ways to write and store your manuscript safely. Your work is automatically saved in the cloud, and you can access it from anywhere—whether you're at home, in a coffee shop, or on your phone in a waiting room.

PENS AND A JOURNAL

Always keep a journal or notebook with you. Ideas come at the most unexpected times, and having a place to jot them down will keep you from forgetting valuable thoughts. Even if you prefer typing, physically writing things down can sometimes help clarify your ideas.

A DIGITAL AUDIO RECORDER (OPTIONAL BUT USEFUL)

If you're someone who processes thoughts better by speaking, an audio recorder can be a lifesaver. You can dictate sections of your book, record ideas while driving, or capture thoughts when writing isn't an option. Most smart phones have built-in recording apps, making this an easy tool to use.

A DEDICATED WRITING SPACE

Having a consistent place to write can help you stay focused. It could be a quiet home office, a local café, or a spot at the library. The key is finding a space that helps you get in the right mindset and minimizes distractions.

A Writing Schedule

Books don't get written by accident. Set aside specific time to write and treat it like an unbreakable appointment. Whether it's an hour before bed, early in the morning, or on weekends, sticking to a routine will help you stay on track. Let those around you know that this is your writing time and that interruptions should be kept to a minimum.

A Trusted Beta Reader

Before sending your manuscript to an editor, let a beta reader take a look. This should be someone who can provide honest, constructive feedback—someone who will tell you what's working and what's not. You don't want someone who will only tell you it's great; you need real insight to improve your book.

An Editor and Proofreader

Editing isn't just about fixing typos—it's about making your writing clearer, more engaging, and structurally sound. An editor will help refine your ideas, while a proofreader will catch any lingering grammar, punctuation, or formatting errors. These professionals will help you present your book in the best possible light.

By gathering these essential resources and committing to a structured writing process, you'll create an environment that supports productivity and progress. Writing a book is a journey, but with the right tools, you can bring your ideas to life and see your manuscript through to completion.

DESTROY YOUR FEAR

I was so worried about going into the 11th grade because in the 11th grade, I knew I would have to write my junior-year term paper. It's been 30 years since I graduated high school, so I don't remember why that term paper was such a big deal, but it was. It was almost like a high school version of a dissertation.

The paper was going to be worth 30% of my grade. The first step of the term paper was to write out the note cards. I was supposed to read the books that I was going to use for my term paper and come up with the topics I was going to write about–I think. It's all a blur.

I put in a half-assed effort and got 20% for that part of the project. I guess that would be like 6% of my total grade. There were four other tasks we were supposed to do along with writing the term paper. I did NONE of them. I was so intimidated by the idea of reading all of those books; I didn't really understand the process and was afraid to ask for help. So I completely failed to do my term paper.

Instead, I studied like crazy for the final exam, made a 98% and passed the class with a 74% total grade. When my teacher called me to the front of the class to show me my final grade in her grade book, she whispered, "You're not going to be able to get away with this next year."

So when I tell you I understand how something so

simple as writing down your thoughts can be so intimidating, I mean it. I wish I'd have had someone who could have helped me overcome my fears, deconstruct the scary walls I had built up in my mind. This is what I want to do for you. So let's shift your perspective on this thing called "writing a book" and destroy the fear wall.

The first swing of the sledge hammer is to let you know that you have already written multiple books. If you have spent any time in school, and especially if you have attended college, you have successfully written a document that could be turned into a book. In high school, how many book reports did you write? How many journals are stacked in your closet? How many love letters have you written?

You've already written a number of books in your life. You just need to change your perspective on what a book really is.

One of my clients came to me with about 80 pages of random journal entries and poems. At first glance, one thing didn't seem to have anything to do with the other. As I got a chance to really talk to her and find out what she wanted to accomplish, the journal entries all began to make sense. She didn't know it at the time, but they were just pieces of a puzzle that we needed to put together.

With a little creativity, transitional stories, embellishment, and a lot of writing time, we carved out a 100-page book that jerked tears and even brought about reconciliation in her family. The point is, if you have words written on pieces of paper, you have the raw material for a published book.

WHAT IS WRITING A BOOK?

Writing a book is nothing more than relaying a message. Ladies, the way you call your girlfriend on the phone to tell her about that crazy situation that happened at work, and you talk for two hours, laughing and enjoying each other–this is the same way you should think about writing a book. Fellas, the way you go to the barber shop and give your opinions on sports or the neighborhood, or joke with the barber–this is the same way you should think about writing a book. You are simply sharing something you have learned or something you have experienced.

Don't make it any more difficult than that. When you sit down to write, imagine yourself talking to your friend and type or write in that vein. Don't think about whether or not the words are grammatically correct. Just get them on paper.

When I coach authors through the writing process, I tell them to think about their first draft like a sculptor with a block of wood. The sculptor starts out chopping huge chunks off of the wood. He is shaping the eyes, the nose, the lips. The sculptor doesn't start with the sandpaper or the refining tools. It's not time for that.

Most writers want the first draft to be what goes to print. They spend hours typing, reading, deleting, rewriting, editing, fine tuning, proofreading, re-reading and after two hours they have only written two paragraphs. Stop it! Your only objective should be getting words on paper. Those words are creating the eyes, nose, lips of the sculpture. They are not ready for refinement, they just need to be chopped out.

WRITING IS NOT AN ELITE SKILL ANYMORE.

Writing used to be special. You have to remember that free public education started in the 1800s. Most people were illiterate and uneducated back then. Education was mainly for the wealthy. So authors of old used lofty and sophisticated literary skills. What could have been stated in three words is extended with grand verbiage. This lent credentials to the author. It positioned him as a master of the language and someone that others should listen to.

Then came Mark Twain dictating his books, using slang and common colloquial language, and the common people loved it. Twain proved you didn't have to be an aristocrat to enjoy literature.

This still holds true. In fact, the average book is written at an eighth-grade reading level. You don't have to be erudite to be a good writer. You don't need a master's degree in English. You simply need to speak to your audience. Your audience speaks your language.

THE BIRTH CYCLE OF YOUR MANUSCRIPT

IDEA!

The moment inspiration strikes, don't doubt or second-guess yourself. ANYTHING can make for a good book if you simply commit to the process.

PREPARATION

This is the time to secure the people, tools, resources, and/or skills necessary to write the book. This could include doing research, outlining, gathering reference materials, or even taking writing courses to improve your skills.

OUTLINING (OPTIONAL BUT RECOMMENDED)

Some writers prefer to "seat-of-the-pants" their way through writing a book (write with no outline)--like myself. However, having a clear structure can make the writing process smoother. This step helps you organize your thoughts and establish the flow of your book.

WRITING (FIRST DRAFT)

Write the first draft of your manuscript. This is a rough, unpolished version, so don't get stuck on perfection. The goal is to get your ideas on paper.

Maybe it's just me, but "write the first draft" sounds like this is something you can do quickly. Your first draft is a process. It may take weeks, months, or possibly years, depending on the complexity of the project. I just want to temper your expectations about how much time your first draft will take.

SELF-REVISION & INITIAL READ-THROUGH

Before handing your manuscript to anyone, take time to review it yourself. Read it from start to finish to catch any major gaps, inconsistencies, or weak points. If necessary, make edits before anyone else sees it.

BETA READING

Give your first draft to beta readers for constructive feedback. You DO NOT want praise at this stage. If someone says your draft is "perfect," get a second opinion. There will always be something you missed, something you didn't consider, or something that needs improvement.

REWRITE (SECOND DRAFT)

Make adjustments, improvements, and embellishments. Fix the problems highlighted by your beta readers. Strengthen weak areas, clarify ideas, and improve flow.

BETA READ/REWRITE CYCLE (AS NEEDED)

Repeat the beta reading and revision process as many times as necessary until you are satisfied with the manuscript. This cycle ensures your book is the best it can be before moving forward.

DEVELOPMENTAL EDITING

Once you have your manuscript written to your satisfaction (or you're just exhausted from revising it), it's time to bring in a developmental editor. They will evaluate your book's structure, flow, logic, pacing, and clarity. They will find holes, inconsistencies, or confusing areas—and they will fix them. Be open to their suggestions!

If you are self-publishing, you have more say in what edits to accept. If you're working with a traditional publisher, their editorial team may have the final say.

LINE EDITING
(Optional, but Recommended for Self-Publishing)

After developmental edits, a line editor fine-tunes the manuscript at the sentence level. They enhance clarity, improve sentence structure, and refine word choice for better readability.

PROOFREADING (FINAL CLEAN-UP)

The proofreader is the house cleaner. They check for correct grammar and punctuation, spot typos, and identify formatting issues. Their job is to make sure your manuscript is polished and error-free before publication.

FINAL APPROVALS & READ-THROUGH

Before approving your book for the next phase, do one final, thorough read-through. At this point, you might be sick of your manuscript, but resist the urge to rush. Read every word carefully.

Congratulations! It's a Baby Manuscript!

LAYING THE GROUNDWORK

THE ANATOMY OF A MANUSCRIPT

The anatomy of a manuscript refers to the structure and components that make up a complete manuscript, from front to back. If you feel overwhelmed wondering about book sections and what order the sections go in, then here is a step-by-step road map of what will make up the anatomy of your manuscript. You don't have to write all of these sections.

FRONT MATTER

The front matter includes all the pages that appear before the main content of the book. These elements help set the stage for the reader.

Title Page: The title page includes the title and subtitle (if any). Space down to the middle of the page, and that is typically where the author's name would go, and the publisher of the book would be at the bottom of the page.

Half Title Page: Some books include a half title page which only includes the book title.

Copyright Page: I typically use this page like the credits of a movie. All of the legal information, copyright, editions, ISBNs, contact information, publisher and contractor information (i.e. photographers or editors who worked on the book) are listed here. All of the small print information about the book is put on the copyright page which is usually directly behind the title page. Your publisher will include copyright information. However, if you're self-publishing, then this is the format of the copyright:

"Copyright © 2025 by Timothy O. Bond.

All rights reserved. No part of this book may be reproduced in any form or by any electronic or mechanical means, including information storage and retrieval or mechanical means without permission in writing from the publisher, except by a reviewer who may quote brief passages in a review."

Dedication: A personal note to dedicate the book to someone. Dedications are not a requirement. If you don't have a specific person to whom you would like to dedicate your book, a good rule of thumb is to dedicate the book to the targeted readers whose lives you would like to impact. A good example:

"This book is dedicated to the men and women who seek to impact the world with their books. May this book inspire and empower you to produce a lasting literary legacy."

Acknowledgments: This is where you can thank people who helped in the process of writing and publishing your book. A word of advice: set specific criteria for earning a mention in the acknowledgments. Don't use acknowledgments to send shout-outs to all of your friends, family, church members and pastors. You open the door for stress and confusion by trying to include your friends in this special moment because if you omit a name, you will hear about it. I've had clients who acknowledged their church and pastors, then left the church and wanted to remove the pastor's name from their book.

Table of Contents: An outline of the chapters and sections in the book, helping readers navigate the structure. Your table of contents only needs to reflect each chapter title. You don't need to include every section and subtitle within the chapter. I've seen tables of contents that were three pages long, because under the title, the author included each subsection.

Foreword/Preface/Introduction: These are all different sections that typically appear at the beginning of a book, but each serves a distinct purpose. Here's a breakdown of the differences between them and their purpose. They are not mandatory. You can have one, you can have all, or you can have none.

Foreword: A foreword is written by someone other than

the author, often an expert, a colleague, or someone influential in the field relevant to the book. Its purpose is to endorse the book, set the tone, and provide credibility by associating the work with a respected figure.

Preface: The preface is written by the author and offers insight into the book's creation. It might describe the inspiration for writing the book, the process, or challenges faced while writing. A preface also helps readers understand the author's intent.

Introduction: The introduction is used to provide an overview of the content of the book, what readers can expect, and sometimes how to read or interpret the book. It's a chance to engage the reader right away.

BODY MATTER

The body matter is the main content of the book and includes all the text and chapters that make up the bulk of the book.

Chapters: These are the primary divisions within the book's narrative or theme. Chapters often include titles or numbers to help the reader follow the structure.

Sections: Larger books are often divided into sections or parts, each containing multiple chapters. If your book explores multiple themes, organizing it into sections can help provide clarity and structure. For example, Section I could include all chapters related to Theme A, Section II would focus on chapters related to Theme B, and so on. This division helps readers easily navigate through different aspects of the book.

Appendices: Additional material like charts, graphs, or supplementary content. Appendices are typically not mandatory for most books, but they can be essential in certain contexts. They are primarily used in nonfiction books that require additional, detailed information that would interrupt the flow of the main content. Here's when appendices might become mandatory:

Academic and Research Books: To provide detailed

data, research findings, or supplementary materials that support the primary content but are too lengthy or specialized to include in the main body.

Legal or Government Documents: To present supplementary materials like laws, regulations, contracts, or policy documents that the book references.

Technical or Instructional Manuals: To provide detailed explanations, instructions, specifications, or additional resources that are important for understanding the primary content.

Nonfiction Books with Extensive Resources: To provide supporting information that readers might want to reference for more in-depth study or practical application, like extensive bibliographies, glossaries, or resource lists.

Notes/Endnotes: Citations or references for sources used within the text.

Notes (footnotes or endnotes) are used to provide additional information, clarifications, citations, or references without interrupting the flow of the main text. They are particularly common in academic, research-based, or nonfiction works. Here's when notes and endnotes might be mandatory:

•Academic or Scholarly Work

•Books with heavy citation requirements

•Legal or medical books

Back Matter

The back matter is the portion of the book after the main text, typically containing supporting or concluding materials.

Glossary: Definitions of specialized terms or jargon used throughout the book. Similar to appendices and notes, there may be books where glossaries are mandatory, but in most personal, nonfiction, memoir-type books, a glossary is not a requirement.

Bibliography: A list of sources and references cited or consulted in the book. Again, not mandatory in most cases.

Index: An alphabetical list of topics, names, or terms mentioned in the book with page references.

About the Author: A brief biography of the author, often including details about their career and other books.
There are two author bios you can write: abbreviated and full. The abbreviated bio is for the back cover. I usually suggest 50 to 75 words for this bio. You have limited space on the back cover. Use your author bio to share a brief background of your credentials, and say why you wrote the book. I personally don't like to see an author share their hobbies and the love they have for their fur

babies. Really? What does that have to do with why I should give you my money to read your book?

Example of a bio by Jack Canfield, world-record holder of most best-selling books:

"Jack Canfield has won numerous awards for his business acumen and marketing genius. He is the co-creator of the Chicken Soup for the Soul Phenomenon."

Short, sweet, and provides ample proof that he is qualified to write his book.

Full bio: This is where you can fill the pages with all of the impressive information you want to add in your biography. This kind of bio usually goes on the last page of the book.

Afterword: A closing section offering final thoughts or insights on the book's themes or impact.

WAYS TO WRITE A MANUSCRIPT

Contrary to popular belief, writing a book no longer means you literally sit down and write a book. As a matter of fact, 90% of books written are not written by the person listed as the author. Of course, I won't be discussing ghostwriting in detail in this book, because if you were using a ghostwriter, then there would be no need for you to have purchased this book, now would there have been?

But as a side note, I will say that ghostwriting is one of the many ways you can write a book. Let someone else do it. Ghostwriters will conduct interviews with you to get an understanding of the ideas, message, and tone you'd like to relay and they will do all of the writing for you.

Ghostwriters can be costly. The average ghostwriter charges in the range of $100 per hour and up. Every hour they spend working on your manuscript is billed. Interviews, writing, editing, researching, making adjustments –it's all billed. Some ghostwriting tabs can run as much as six figures.

WRITING VS. SPEAKING

I'm a writer. I write better than I speak. When I'm speaking, I stumble over my words, forget words and names in my mind. But when I'm writing, I have a better grasp of my word bank and how to use it. I can sit down and write thousands of words in a few hours. It just flows out. Perhaps you're like me. If so, then you get satisfaction in painting words on your literary canvas.

However, there are people who speak better than they write. I've spoken to people who can't seem to get three words on a piece of paper, but if you asked them what they wanted to write about, they could give you the most inspiring and motivational explanation of what they want to write, replete with examples, details, and funny stories.

For that person, they should speak their manuscript–record their thoughts and ideas and allow someone to transcribe the words for them, or use a speak-to-text application.

WHAT ABOUT AI?

Sigh...

Okay, let's talk about this AI craze. I'll be upfront and admit that I am biased against AI because I believe it is quickly taking away our ability to think and create. Yet I have also found it useful.

Let's talk about it.

AI IS STEALING OUR CREATIVITY.

When AI came out and I realized the potential it offered as an author, I was intrigued. I thought of how such a tool could aid writers and publishers. I was working on a book and decided to play with it. I typed in commands such as:

"Write 500 words about the impact of the church in American politics. Write it like Martin Luther King talks."

It was fun. As time went on, I began to use it for more and more tasks. Then one day, I decided to sit down and start working on my new book, *Becoming a Legacy Author,* and my first inclination was to pull up AI. My brain felt empty, as if I was disconnected from my gift of writing. I realized at that moment that if I allowed it to happen, I would trade my voice for that of artificial intelligence.

When I took a step back, I started to realize that the AI voice is a dead and soulless voice. AI is an effective tool to relay ideas, but it does not relay a message.

When I was a kid in church, playing in the back, my mom would look back and give me "the look." She didn't say a word, but I got the *message*. *A message is transferred through emotion and spirit. AI has no spirit, and when you read AI writing, you can feel the coldness in the writing. Even in its best attempt, there's just something missing.*

LEGALITIES OF AI

Concerning the legal protections of using AI, I still have questions. AI is a massive amalgamation of data collected across the World Wide Web; however, I question the inimitability of the output an AI manuscript provides. The response of AI is contingent upon how we instruct the AI program. As of today, ChatGPT has over 100 million users. Full disclosure, I just got that information from ChatGPT.

I find it hard to believe that for 100 million people, AI is spitting out completely unique and tailored answers. I find it hard to believe that there would not be some form of overlap in the requests and algorithms that make up the manuscripts people are creating using AI. The question is, how do we protect IP (intellectual property) when the property did not come from our intellect?

How You Should Use AI as a Writer

There are two productive–and dare I say ethical–ways to use AI, in my opinion.

Editing and Proofreading: AI is a great tool for editing and proofreading your books. Sorry editors, but we need to pivot, because those jobs are gone! What used to take editors hours to do can now be done in seconds. AI has the ability to sharpen your worst writing and will tell you everything it did and why.

I will usually prompt AI to "proofread and improve where necessary."

When using AI editing and proofreading, I warn you to be very attentive. At this time (2025), AI is still learning. I've found some errors it did not catch, and instances where it made a sentence worse. Also, don't get in the habit of simply cutting and pasting big chunks of text. Copy and paste enough to be able to glance at the result and catch any possible issues.

I have found that somehow, the program forgets what I've asked it to do and starts commenting on the text that I have asked it to proofread.

If you're just cutting and pasting, you may look up to find a completely different manuscript than you submitted to AI.

Breaking through writer's block and writing prompts: I use AI when I'm struggling with writer's block and need writing prompts. When you get to a point in your writing process when you don't know what else to say, ask AI if it sees any areas where your manuscript can be improved. It will spit out a list of topics and approaches that you could take with the manuscript. Take those and use your own intellect to structure your opinion and response.

Essentially, I don't see anything wrong with using AI to enhance your message, but I have a problem with authors who believe they have somehow hacked the game, and who allow AI to be their voice.

10 DON'TS OF MANUSCRIPT WRITING

1. Don't set an illogical timeframe

Writing a book is like building a house—you never know what might come up and throw off your timeline. A good rule of thumb is to give yourself 3-6 months to write your book. We'll discuss how to set a writing schedule and word count in later chapters.

2. Don't edit while you write

We'll dive deeper into this later, but here's the key: fight the urge to edit each line immediately after writing it. I've found that a manuscript writes itself—you're just the conduit. Editing as you go might change important details or ruin the flow of your ideas before you've completed the full draft. Don't EDIT Flow...LET IT Flow. (I know, it's a little corny, but it works.)

3. Don't try to be perfect

This will be mentioned several times throughout the book, and that's because it's the biggest challenge for most writers. Many want to present a perfect manuscript on the first try. I even have clients who try to edit their manuscript before handing it to the editor. You're paying the editor to fix problems—let them do their job.

4. Don't get stuck in preparation

I know people who have been "preparing" to write a

If you don't have the skill or desire, there are others who can do it for you.

book for decades. But too much preparation can become an excuse for procrastination. If you've been preparing for more than a week, it's time to stop planning and start writing.

5. Don't compare your writing to others

Your writing style is your voice. It's okay to be inspired by an author you admire, but never compare your work to someone else's. You have your own unique story to tell.

6. Don't try to format the book

I know you're eager to see your book in its finished form, but if you're not a graphic designer, typesetter, or equipped with the proper software, you're just creating frustration by trying to format your manuscript yourself. Leave that to the professionals. Attempting it yourself can lead to issues with conversion, spacing, and other headaches for the typesetter.

7. Don't consider your book "your baby"

Your book is not your baby. It's a collection of words and ideas. Stop trying to protect your ego and focus on creating something impactful. If you truly care about the quality of your manuscript, you'll be willing to hand it over for critique, even if it means ripping it apart and putting it back together again.

8. Don't be defensive over your manuscript

Here's a hard truth: if a reader finds your writing confusing, it's because it is. Just because you know what you meant doesn't mean it's translating clearly on the page. Trust your readers, and be open to feedback.

9. Don't seek validation

Just because you're excited about writing a book doesn't mean everyone else will be. I once had someone ask me "Did God speak to you about me writing a book?" They were looking for a sign. If you're waiting for validation from others, you might be disappointed when you get that first blank stare from someone who doesn't even own a bookshelf. Write the book because you believe in it. You don't need anyone else's approval. Anything can be successful if you commit to the process.

10. Don't fill your manuscript with fluff

Focus on quality, not quantity. Readers can tell when you're padding your manuscript just to make it longer. Your page count won't make your book more valuable. In fact, in today's world of short attention spans and social media, a bulky book might even work against you. Aim for concise, impactful content that leaves readers wanting more. We'll go over tips to help you write a great manuscript later, so keep reading!

WRITING A GREAT

MANUSCRIPT

FACTS TELL; STORIES SELL

Imagine you've just spent your hard-earned money to see a movie. You walk into the theater expecting to be entertained—expecting to laugh, cry, feel angry, get sad, and then eventually find joy by the end. You settle in, the lights dim, and the screen comes to life. But instead of watching the characters unfold and the plot develop, there stands a man in the center of the screen, delivering a long, dry lecture about the plot—telling you everything that's happening in the movie, but with no emotion, no sense of pacing, and no action. It's just a string of facts, delivered in a monotonous tone. How long would you stay in your seat? And how soon would you be demanding a refund?

This scenario sounds ridiculous, doesn't it? And yet, it's exactly what many writers do. Whether you're writing a book, an article, a speech, or any other piece of content, if you're simply presenting facts, you're likely to lose your audience's attention quickly.

Unless you're writing a technical manual, your job is to entertain your reader. If you don't, you'll lose them in a matter of pages. And it happens more than you think. In a survey of book buyers, 52% of readers admitted they only read about half of the books they purchase. That means that more than half of readers put books down before reaching the end. The truth is, even the most well-written factual book will fall short if it's not engaging.

So, what's the secret to holding a reader's attention? The answer is simple: stories.

Stories are powerful because they capture the reader's imagination and emotions. People relate to characters, situations, and emotions in stories because they see themselves in them. A well-told story connects on a personal level, drawing the reader in and keeping them engaged. When you tell a story, your audience doesn't just read your words—they experience them.

If you're writing fiction, you're already doing this—you're telling a story. But what about nonfiction? How do you keep readers engaged when you're trying to communicate ideas, lessons, or facts? It's easy to fall into the trap of drowning the reader in endless facts, statistics, and dry details. But if you do that, you risk losing them halfway through the first chapter.

Instead of just presenting facts, immerse your reader in stories that help them understand and internalize your message. A great nonfiction writer uses storytelling to make their points come alive. Whether you're sharing personal anecdotes, case studies, or real-life examples, stories are the vehicle that will allow you to convey your message in a way that resonates with your audience. Let your stories guide the reader toward their own conclusions, allowing them to feel the experience rather than just be told the facts.

As the saying goes, "Never make a point without telling a story, and never tell a story without making a point." This is the key to creating a lasting connection with your readers. A story without a point is simply entertainment, and a point without a story is just information. But when you combine them, you have a compelling, unforgettable narrative that both entertains and educates.

In the end, your readers are looking for more than just information—they're looking for an experience. So, whether you're writing fiction or nonfiction, don't forget to tell a story. Make it real, make it emotional, and make it impactful. When you do, you'll find that not only will your readers stay engaged, but they'll be coming back for more.

D.N.A.

How do I make my manuscript compelling?

I'm glad you asked. Well-written manuscripts for any genre consist of three components that we call the DNA of a manuscript. Just as DNA is what creates our characteristics, features, and some even believe our personalities, the DNA of a manuscript is what brings the manuscripts to life.

D is for Dialogue

Instead of telling the reader what was said, allow them to experience the conversation firsthand. Well-crafted dialogue creates engagement, emotion, and realism. Good dialogue should be natural and engaging. It should sound like real speech. There's nothing worse than reading a manuscript where people speak with perfect grammar and the characters sound like they are giving a presentation to the board of directors.

"Hello, James. It is so pleasing to see you today. Did you have a great morning?"

Who talks like that? No one I know.

N is for Narrative

Narrative moves the manuscript along. It's like the trolley taking you through the literary experience. Narrative provides context, description, and insight. It includes inner thoughts, world-building, and transitions between scenes. Narrative should set the tone and mood and give depth to characters' thoughts and emotions.

Avoid excessive telling, and **show** the reader rather than tell them.

A is for Action

Your manuscript needs some action. Action keeps the story exciting and immediate. It includes physical movement, suspense, and real-time reactions. Good action is clear and concise—no unnecessary words. It matches the pacing of the scene (fast for intense moments, slower for tension-building), and it involves sensory details to immerse the reader.

Here are examples of a sentence with no DNA and one with DNA:

No DNA:

"Mark and Sam were in a dark place. Mark was scared because it was cold and unsettling. He thought something might be inside, but Sam didn't seem as worried."

This sentence just tells the raw facts of what is happening. The story is frozen in this moment of time with no action. When you think about this sentence, what do you see in your mind? I just see two avatars standing frozen in front of an open door.

Same scene with DNA:

"Do you feel that?" Mark whispered, his breath shallow (**D**). His heart pounded as he stared into the darkness beyond the open door. The cold air from inside wrapped around him like an unseen hand, pulling him forward (**N**). He took a shaky step closer, his fingers grazing the edge of the doorframe (**A**).

This keeps the tension high while blending all three elements naturally. When writing, give your manuscript life with DNA.

SHOW, DON'T TELL

Readers don't just want to read your words—they want to **feel** them. They want to step into your world, breathe its air, hear its sounds, and taste its flavors. Great storytelling isn't just about telling a story; it's about showing it in a way that pulls the reader in and makes them feel like they are experiencing it firsthand.

One of the most powerful ways to achieve this is through sensory language. Sensory language is the use of words that engage the five senses:

•**Sight** – What does the character see? Colors, shapes, movement, shadows, or light?

•**Hearing** – What sounds fill the environment? Silence, whispers, echoes, distant laughter, or a sudden crash?

•**Touch** – What textures or temperatures are present? Smooth silk, rough bark, icy wind, or the comforting warmth of a fire?

•**Smell** – What scents linger in the air? Fresh rain, burning wood, blooming flowers, or the sharp tang of saltwater?

•**Taste** – What flavors are present? Sweet honey, bitter coffee, tangy citrus, or the spiced heat of cinnamon?

By weaving these sensory details into your writing, you create a richer, more immersive experience for the reader. Using sensory details in your writing:

•**Creates vivid imagery** – Helps the reader visualize scenes clearly.

•**Elicits emotional responses** – Connects readers to characters and settings.

•**Enhances realism** – Makes the story feel authentic and believable.

•**Engages the reader** – Draws them in and keeps them turning the pages.

Let's look at an example:

Basic sentence (telling, not showing):
"Sarah walked into the kitchen and felt happy."
This tells us what's happening, but it doesn't make us feel anything. Now, let's enhance it with sensory details:

Sensory-rich sentence (showing the experience):
"The warm scent of cinnamon and baked apples filled the air as Sarah stepped into the cozy kitchen. The wooden floor was smooth and cool beneath her bare feet. A golden glow from the flickering candlelight danced on

the walls, casting soft shadows. Outside, raindrops tapped gently against the window, their rhythmic pitter-patter blending with the crackling of logs in the fire-place. She reached for a fresh slice of apple pie, its flaky crust crumbling at her touch, and took a bite—sweet, spiced perfection that melted on her tongue."

Now, let's break it down by sense:

•**Sight:** *A golden glow from the flickering candlelight danced on the walls, casting soft shadows.*

•**Hearing:** *Outside, raindrops tapped gently against the window, their rhythmic pitter-patter blending with the crackling of logs in the fireplace.*

•**Touch:** *The wooden floor was smooth and cool beneath her bare feet.*

•**Smell:** *The warm scent of cinnamon and baked apples filled the air.*

•**Taste:** *She reached for a fresh slice of apple pie, its flaky crust crumbling at her touch, and took a bite—sweet, spiced perfection that melted on her tongue.*

Each sense adds depth to the scene, making it vivid and immersive rather than flat and forgettable.

PRACTICE EXERCISE

Try transforming these basic sentences into sensory-rich experiences:

1. *The forest was quiet.*
2. *He drank his coffee.*
3. *The beach was hot.*
4. *She was nervous before the test.*
5. *Dinner was delicious.*

Think about each of the five senses and how they might enhance these moments. What sounds, textures, smells, tastes, and sights can you add?

Sensory language is one of the most powerful tools a writer can use to captivate readers. The more you practice incorporating sensory details into your writing, the more immersive and engaging your storytelling will become. Instead of merely telling your story, make your readers feel it.

Now, grab your pen (or keyboard) and bring your words to life!

_____

_____

_____

_____

_____

_____

_____

_____

_____

_____

_____

_____

_____

_____

_____

_____

_____

_____

_____

_____

_____

_____

_____

_____

_____

_____

_____

_____

_____

If you don't have the skill or desire, there are others who can do it for you. | 55

Timothy O. Bond

STAYING ON TRACK

CREATING A WRITING SCHEDULE

In 2007, I worked with a guy who told me he wanted me to publish his book. He said he had the outline and would get back with me when he was finished writing. In 2010, I spoke with him again. He had an outline, and was going to get serious and connect with me again. In 2015 I spoke with him again. He laughed, and he told me he was still serious and would get with me. In 2023, he called me and is still wanting to write this book.

It is 2025, 18 years later; 6,570 days since he first told me he wanted to write a book. If he had only written five words a day, he would have enough words to have published his book.

Writing a book is not hard; you just have to sit down and write. Bill Gates said, "Most people overestimate what they can do in a year and underestimate what they can do in 10 years." Most people sit down with good intentions to write. They think they will sit down in a day and write 50,000 perfect words. When they face reality, they give up instead of simply accepting that the process will take a little longer.

If you commit to a schedule of regular writing–no matter how long or short the writing sessions are–you will experience more progress than you could fathom.

My client Krissi Quarles had never written a book. She had only a few journal entries, so she was literally starting from scratch. But she committed to the process of weekly coaching sessions and writing three days a week in between. Within six weeks, Krissi completed a nearly 300-page book.

Check out her story:

 https://youtu.be/zcYpF2a9PaQ? si=MwANb2914JTuMZG-

SYSTEM OVER SKILL

It's a matter of system over skill. You don't have to know what you're doing; you just need to follow the system. If you write a page per day for 30 days, you will have a 30-page manuscript in a month. You will have raw material that your editors, proofreaders, coaches, and friends can help you refine. You don't have to be perfect, you just need to be consistent.

A few things to consider when creating your writing schedule:

WHERE YOU WILL WRITE:

Environment impacts your success. Most people pay for a gym membership because that's where they are inspired. You can run around your neighborhood. You don't need the treadmill at the Planet Fitness that is 10 miles from your house. You go there because it is an environment that encourages fitness. Your writing environment should encourage your writing. If you have to carve out a little nook in your home where you can get away from your kids and spouse for 20 minutes of peace, or if you have to drive to the closest Starbucks to feel like a true writer, do it.

WHAT TIME YOU WILL WRITE:

Write when you are most creative. Waiting until you have finished a grueling work day is not the best time to write, UNLESS writing is how you calm down. Choose a writing time when you can focus on nothing but your writing. I guess it goes without saying that this is not television time. Some of you may have to wake up an hour early or go to sleep an hour later. Some may have to use their work break and lunch times. Instead of sitting in the car scarfing down those mystery meat chicken nuggets, get your words on paper.

One lady shared that she woke up at 4:00 in the morning, hours before her children and husband woke up, so that she could get a couple of hours of writing in. Another man wrote only after putting the entire family to sleep. Is it a sacrifice? Yes.

WHAT DAYS YOU WILL WRITE:

Perhaps you can write every day, but if you can't that is completely fine. Write four days a week, three, or even one, as long as you commit to that day. Perhaps your weekends are your only free days. Let Saturday and Sunday be your writing days. Commit to a specific amount of time on those days.

HOW LONG YOU WILL WRITE:

Don't be lazy and set a 20- minute writing goal, knowing that you have the entire day off. Be professional and give it a true commitment. If you don't have to sacrifice something to make it happen, then you're not really trying.

Give yourself enough time to get into a flow. During the first few minutes of most writing sessions, you'll need to reboot your writing engine. You may sit for a few minutes, type three words and immediately delete them. It takes time to get into a flow, but it will come. Only you know how long that flow takes. Give yourself adequate time.

HOW MANY WORDS YOU WANT TO TYPE:

This is not a requirement, but it could give you an extra boost to have an actual writing goal. I often give myself word count goals. I know if I can write at least 500 words per session, I'm making good progress. Just so you know, 500 words is one full page. I usually write more than that, but the mind trick of one page allows me to walk away with a win every time I write.

Don't get restricted by this word count. Even the

best writers have days when getting only five words on paper was a HUGE victory.

MAKE THE COMMITMENT BELOW:

I commit to write _____ hours per day, _____ day(s) per week.

I will write on the following day(s)

_____

I will write from:_____am / pm until _____ am / pm.

I will write at

_____

_____ (location), free from distraction.

I will write _____ words per session.

LET'S WRITE

FRAMEWORK FOR WRITING NONFICTION

Let me preface these steps by explaining that this information is mostly useful for nonfiction books, but some of the tactics can also be used for fiction.

If I had a dime for every time an aspiring writer asked me, "What's the process?" I'd be a rich man. I believe they are asking how to approach the writing process. Is there a framework? Are there steps? Is it like the term papers in high school where we had to first write out note cards, then write out an outline, then blah, blah, blah...? Remember, I didn't do my term paper.

To this I say, FORGET ALL OF THAT! No, I'm kidding. Here is my framework for writing your manuscript.

MANUSCRIPT STRUCTURE

When it comes to structuring the length of paragraphs, chapters, and word counts, there are no hard-and-fast rules. However, understanding some general guidelines can make your manuscript more polished and effective. Let's break it down.

PARAGRAPHS: HOW MANY TO EXPLAIN A POINT

One of my biggest pet peeves is getting a manuscript from an author that looks like a 100-page paragraph. Unless you are using a highly complex doctorate-level writing style, there's no reason your paragraphs should be 15 lines of text. Here are some standard rules. Some characteristics of paragraphs:

Short and Concise: Each paragraph should focus on a single idea. Typically, keep paragraphs between three and five sentences. If your point is simple and straightforward, your paragraph could be just one or two sentences. If you're telling a story about how Jane went to the store to buy coffee, then paragraph one should be about Jane going to the store, and paragraph two will be about her buying coffee.

Complex Points: For more detailed or layered topics, your paragraphs can run six to ten sentences, or more. The key is to avoid overly long, dense paragraphs. Break them up when needed to keep things readable. Usually, I find most ideas are fully fleshed out in four to five paragraphs.

Purpose of Paragraphs: Each paragraph serves as a step in your argument or story. If you're building a case, each one should flow logically into the next, leading to the conclusion or next development.

Word Count: How Many Words Should a Chapter Contain?

On average, chapters usually range from 1,500 to 5,000

words, but this can vary depending on your genre and writing style. I would not be too strict about word count, but I would also suggest not being too lenient. One page of formatted text is not sufficient to be considered a chapter. You may want to consider adding that page as a section to a bigger chapter. Here are a few tips on chapters:

Short Chapters: In fast-paced genres (like thrillers or young adult), chapters often fall between 1,500 to 2,500 words.

Longer Chapters: Literary fiction, nonfiction, and epic novels typically have chapters between 3,000 to 5,000 words.

How Many Words To Make Your Point: In nonfiction, chapters should focus on a single, clear point. Typically, this means your chapter will range from 2,500 to 4,000 words to cover the topic in depth. However, the real measure should be how much material is needed to communicate your idea fully.

Cliffhangers/Engagement: Fiction chapters, especially those with tension or cliffhangers, tend to be shorter—around 1,500 to 2,000 words—because you want to keep the pace quick and engaging.

GENERAL GUIDELINES FOR CHAPTER ORGANIZATION

Introduction: Every chapter should have a clear beginning. This could be a hook, a question raised, or a problem introduced. In nonfiction, it's often an idea or premise that sets the tone for the chapter.

Development: The body of the chapter should develop the main point, story, or argument. This part will make up the bulk of your chapter and move the narrative forward. It's where you build ideas, introduce new concepts, or create tension.

Conclusion: Every chapter needs some kind of closure. Even if it's a cliffhanger that leads into the next chapter, there should be a resolution of some sort. In nonfiction, you might end with a summary or a call to action; in fiction, it could be a resolution or something that leaves readers on the edge of their seats.

PACING AND READABILITY

Mixing Up Lengths: One of the best ways to keep your writing engaging is by varying paragraph and sentence lengths. Shorter paragraphs create urgency, keeping the pace quick. Longer ones can slow things down and allow readers to absorb more information. By mixing things up, you create a rhythm that helps maintain your readers' interest.

Action vs. Reflection: When you're writing a fast-paced chapter (think action or tension), shorter paragraphs (50-100 words) work well. For slower moments, when you want to dig into emotions or explore a concept, longer paragraphs (150-300 words) help maintain a reflective tone.

The structure of your manuscript should serve your story and keep the reader engaged. Use these guidelines to create a smooth flow, but focus on clarity and readability, not on sticking rigidly to word counts. Each paragraph should build your argument or narrative, and each chapter should move the story forward. With the right balance of pacing, detail, and readability, your manuscript will come together as a compelling, cohesive work.

BRAINSTORMING

First, we're going to start by brainstorming every-thing you want to talk about in your book. Opinions may differ on this. Some people need a strict outline that gives them a roadmap. If that is how your brain works best, then use these same instructions with your outline. For me, I like the journey. I like to get lost in the creative process, dump all of the metaphorical puzzle pieces on the table and figure out what goes where.

Trust me, this process can be incredibly freeing. When I wrote my second book, *Fall In Love with the Struggle,* it felt like a download straight from my mind to the page. It was as if the entire book came to me in an instant. Ideas were pouring in—so many topics, lessons, and stories I wanted to share. The thoughts were bounc-ing around in my head like a ping-pong ball, each one competing for my attention. It was exhilarating but also overwhelming.

I decided to do a brainstorming session. I grabbed a blank piece of paper, no distractions, just me and my thoughts. And I started writing—everything that came to mind, without holding back.

"You have to mess up to clean up."

"Struggles vs. snags."\

"Struggle is God's most useful tool."

No rhyme, no reason, no order—just a stream of consciousness spilling out onto the paper. The point was to get everything out that I wanted to share, no matter how it looked. I didn't know what chapter these topics would fit into. Heck, I didn't even know if some of them belonged in the book at all. All I knew was that I wanted to write about those topics.

This is your starting point. Begin by writing down everything you want to share with your audience. Do not worry about organizing it at this stage. Let the ideas flow freely—just write everything down, no matter how scattered it may seem. This is the stage where you need to unleash your thoughts. Don't hold back. If it's important to you, write it down. If you think it will resonate with your audience, write it down.

You may feel overwhelmed at first, but that's okay. This is part of the process. Keep writing until you feel like you've emptied yourself out. You'll know when that happens—it's a palpable feeling when your mind feels clear and your ideas have been fully expressed. That's when you know you've done enough. It's like a weight lifted off your chest.

Once you've written everything down, you can move to the next step: writing the actual content. And here's a crucial tip—don't worry about the order of things. Start with the topic that excites you the most. Inspiration comes and goes, so it's important to write when you feel inspired. The worst thing you can do is force yourself to write in a particular order. One day, you might get a few paragraphs into chapter one, but the next day, you may be on fire about chapter eight. Don't let rigid structure stunt your progress. The key is to get the words on the page, even if they're not in the right place yet.

Progress is progress, no matter where it happens in the book. If you're writing, you're moving forward, and that's what matters most. Don't get bogged down by the small stuff—just keep the momentum going. Eventually, you'll start to see how the pieces fall into place.

Use this blank section to brainstorm the topics you want to address in your book. It doesn't matter if they seem random at first. It doesn't matter if you don't know how everything fits together. Just get it out. The organization and structure will come later, but for now, your only job is to let the ideas flow. Your first draft is just that—a draft. It doesn't need to be perfect.

Allow yourself to dream big and not to worry about the details just yet. This is your creative phase—let your mind roam free. It's time to dive in.

_____

_____

_____

_____

_____

_____

_____

_____

_____

_____

_____

_____

_____

_____

_____

_____

_____

_____

_____

_____

_____

_____

_____

_____

_____

_____

_____

_____

_____

If you don't have the skill or desire, there are others who can do it for you. | 75

Good morning!

I'm assuming you slept on all of the topics you wrote down yesterday and one of those topics really started talking to you, right?

I just want to remind you that the heading of this section is "Choose your topic...for the day." You may have no excitement for this topic tomorrow. If that happens don't waste your time or energy fighting with your muse. Work with your inspiration, not against it. Writing should feel fluid, not forced. If a certain topic isn't coming naturally, don't waste time trying to force it. Instead, shift your focus to a subject that excites and energizes you. Inspiration fuels creativity, and when you write from a place of passion, your words will flow more effortlessly, making the writing process enjoyable.

Here are a few helpful tips to help you during your writing sessions:

THINK PRODUCTIVITY OVER PERFECTION

Imagine your friend asks you to walk with him to your favorite ice cream parlor. Your mouth is watering for that delicious ice cream, but after three steps, your friend stops, turns around, and walks back to make sure he locked the door.

Okay, the door is locked. You start walking again. Your friend stops again. "Do you think I locked the door well enough?" You argue over the way he locked the door for five minutes and he agrees to keep moving.

You take another few steps and he stops and takes five backward steps. "I didn't like the way my feet turned when I took those last three steps, I wanted to do those over."

You're probably feeling the agitation in your chest right now. Well, this is how most people write. They get so bogged down and obsessive over the most trivial issues with the manuscript that they can never move forward. Fight the urge to reread your writing, fix errors, typos, punctuation, or any other nitpicky issues that you may find. This is one of the biggest roadblocks to progress. Remember the sculptor. This is not the time for refinement. Focus on progress and not perfection.

TAP INTO YOUR PASSION

Napoleon Hill wrote the best-selling book Think and Grow Rich. Many of the most successful businessmen and businesswomen attribute their success to this book. However, there's a little secret people don't know: when he first put the book out, it did not sell very well. After reading the book, Hill said he realized that he didn't write it in the right spirit. He rewrote the entire book, word by word, but the second time, he wrote it with the spirit of passion and conviction that he believed he wanted to relay to his audience, and the book took off from there.

Although I am stressing the importance of getting words on paper, I think it is just as important to tap into the passion and conviction for your topic that you want your reader to assimilate. I often tell my clients that if they don't laugh, cry, get angry, or feel happy while writing their books, then their audience won't feel those emotions either. I have found this to be true with every client I have worked with.

Take the time before you start writing to get yourself charged up into the emotional state of your topic, whether it be joy, anger, sadness, fear, or boldness. Whatever emotion charged you up so profoundly and influenced you to take on this endeavor of writing a book, that should be the emotion that flows from your pages into the mind of the reader.

HONOR YOUR CREATIVE PROCESS

Everyone's writing journey is different, and recognizing what works best for you will make the process more fulfilling. Just as you wouldn't stay in a place where you aren't appreciated, don't force yourself into a creative space that doesn't feel right. Lean into the flow of your ideas and give yourself permission to follow the path of least resistance. Writing should be a process of discovery, not a battle.

There will be times when it seems like you are running off on a tangent while writing. You will think, "This is worthless" and be tempted to delete what you've written. I'll tell you what I tell my clients: never delete anything. Instead, if you find that you have written content that doesn't quite fit, cut and paste it at the bottom of your document in a section that you will label "Basement."

Anything that doesn't seem to fit goes in the basement for storage. I discovered this practice while working with my first manuscript coaching client. There were so many good paragraphs, concepts and ideas that didn't seem to fit anywhere. Instead of deleting them, we put them in the basement, and lo and behold, as we further developed the manuscript, we were able to go back into the basement and pull content that fit better in other areas.

It's always better to have too much content and have to trim, than to not have enough content and have to add. So don't judge your writing process. If words are flowing, let them flow. You can trim fat later.

EVERYTHING IS CONNECTED

If you are writing your personal story, remember that everything is connected. You may think that you are writing random stories during this process, but everything that you have experienced is a part of one story. That story is what created the person you are today. So that story about how you got lost in the grocery store may seem random, but as you delve deeper into your story, you will find out how that experience shaped your entire approach to life and how your life has turned out.

ALLOW YOUR WRITING TO BE YOUR THERAPY

"I can't do this anymore!" my client yelled into the phone in a tearful panic.

I was used to it. Without fail, my coaching clients get to a place where they shut down access. They write something bland like, "My mother and I had a complicated relationship" and then attempt to slide on past that statement like it was black ice. Noooo! I don't let that slide. When you're writing a book, especially one about your life, you are inviting people into the inner sanctum of your experience. You are either all in or not. I'm going to encourage you to really open up.

You have to open up and go into those dark recesses. The memories you have chosen to bury, the emotions you forgot you had. This is a part of the process of writing a book. It's not just for the accomplishment, not just for the money–it's also an opportunity for healing.

During the writing of another client's book, we realized that she needed to interview her father to get more clarity about his perspective on the day she and her sister were taken from him and put in foster care. As they discussed the issue, she revealed information to her father about that day that he never knew. For decades he had believed his ex-wife had called the authorities on him out of spite, when in actuality, the author had cut herself while her father was away at work and when they sought help from a neighbor and called 911, the state stepped in and treated the case like a child neglect case.

My point is, while writing your book, you may find yourself opening some emotional doors that you would rather keep shut. I implore you to step in and address those issues and allow the writing of your book to bring therapy and healing.

THE HOOK (STEP 1)

The scene opens. Rick Grimes and Daryl Dixon plunge into a dark pit. Rick flicks his cigarette lighter, its small flame barely cutting through the shadows. Suddenly—a rotting face lunges at him. A zombie. He stumbles back, kicking the creature away, only to realize they're not alone. More are closing in, their ravenous moans echoing off the walls. There's no way out.

The screen goes black. Theme music plays.

I was hooked.

I got addicted to The Walking Dead series, and over time, I understood the method to their madness: they didn't ease viewers into the action—they threw them into it. Every episode opened at the peak of tension. The characters were trapped, backs against the wall, no escape in sight. Doom felt inevitable. I started the show with intense emotions and ended the show in the same way. I found myself binge-watching it for literally hours and even full days because of the hooks and cliffhangers.

As much as possible, your chapters should be as addictive. Start with a hook—a story, a sentence, a phrase, or even a single word that grabs the reader's attention and demands they keep going. And then—take them to the beginning.

82 | If you don't have the skill or desire, there are others who can do it for you.

A great hook forces the reader to turn the page. Maybe you didn't realize it, but I hooked you with that first paragraph. By starting with "The scene opens," I immediately pulled you into the action. For a split second, you may have thought, Wait, is this a movie? A show? What's happening? That curiosity—that need to know more—is what makes a great hook.

Here are a few ways to create a good hook for your chapters:

START WITH A BOLD STATEMENT OR THOUGHT-PROVOKING QUESTION

Begin your chapter with a sentence that makes the reader stop and think. A surprising fact, a controversial opinion, or a deep question immediately pulls them in. Example: "What if I told you that everything you've been taught about success is a lie?" This type of opening makes readers curious and eager to find out more.

DROP THE READER INTO THE ACTION

Instead of easing into the scene, start in the middle of something happening. Action creates urgency and engages readers from the first sentence. Example: "The tires screeched as I yanked the wheel, narrowly missing the guardrail." By immediately placing the reader in the moment, they feel compelled to keep going and find out what happens next.

Timothy O. Bond

Use a Vivid, Unexpected Description

Paint a picture with words that evoke emotion and create intrigue. Strong imagery can make a reader feel like they've stepped into your world. Example: "The room smelled of regret and cheap whiskey, a combination that clung to the faded curtains like an old memory." This kind of sensory detail draws the reader in and makes them want to explore the world you're creating.

THE ORIGIN STORY (STEP 2)

Once you've hooked your reader, it's time to give them the origin story. This is where you dive deeper into the journey of how you acquired the knowledge you're about to share. As authors, we share our insights from one of two places: they come from what we've learned or from what we've earned.

What we've learned comes from the wisdom of others: books, mentors, or experts. What we've earned, on the other hand, is knowledge we've gained through personal experiences. *Side note: I learned that concept from Russell Brunson.*

Whether you're sharing learned or earned knowledge, there is one thing that ties them together: the origin story. This is the story of how you acquired this knowledge—where your life was before you knew what you now know, how your life transformed after attaining that knowledge, and why you believe it's essential for your readers to understand it. An origin story isn't just a backstory; it's the bridge that connects your reader to the transformation that awaits them if they choose to embrace the knowledge you're about to share.

The origin story is powerful because it humanizes the message, making it more relatable. People connect with people, not ideas. When I wrote my second book, people told me, "I couldn't put it down." One reader told me, "I don't read. This is the first book I've read from front to back. I read it in one night."

The reason they couldn't put the book down was because the book is full of stories. Personal stories that they could empathize and/or sympathize with. They wanted to know how I overcame the challenges I wrote about.

Maybe you're saying, "I don't have any good stories." Not to worry, you don't have to be the focus of the origin story. The origin story can be someone else's story or a random situation. Think of it as a collection of life-changing experiences—either your own or others'—that collectively show the reader the transformative power of the knowledge you're presenting.

A great example of this type of storytelling can be found in the works of Malcolm Gladwell. In his book *The Tipping Point,* Gladwell uses stories to illustrate his points. For instance, Gladwell begins The Tipping Point with the fascinating origin story of the Hush Puppies shoe brand. The story isn't just about shoes—it's about how small, seemingly insignificant events can create massive shifts. Gladwell goes on to tell the stories of television producers, actresses, a skateboard company, and more. Each story is a piece of evidence that supports his overarching thesis while also entertaining the reader with real, engaging examples.

This blend of education and entertainment is not just about conveying facts—it's about delivering those facts through stories that captivate the reader's imagination and keep them turning the pages. As an author, you want to use your origin story–whether it's your own or someone else's, or a random situation–to engage your reader's emotions and curiosity, making the knowledge you share not just something they understand, but something they feel.

Remember, the origin story is not just about you—it's about the journey from where your reader is now to where you want them to be. When they read your story, they should see themselves in it, and they should be able to picture how their life could be different once they acquire the knowledge you're offering. You're not just educating them; you're inspiring them to take action.

Now it's time to take your knowledge and frame it within the context of a story that will engage, entertain, and most importantly, transform your reader. The origin story is where the real magic happens. It's where you connect the dots between where your reader is now and where they could be, all thanks to the wisdom you've earned (or learned) and are passing along to them.

MAKE YOUR POINT (CONCLUSION)

HOW TO EFFECTIVELY DRIVE YOUR POINTS HOME

Once you've told your story—using strong narrative structure and sensory language to bring it to life—it's time to drive your points home. A compelling story lays the foundation, but how you present your key takeaways determines how well they resonate with your readers.

Here are three effective ways to structure your points, along with examples:

1. End with a Powerful Conclusion

Wrap up your chapter with one clear, overarching takeaway. This approach reinforces the core message of your story, leaving a lasting impression on the reader.

Example:

Imagine you've told a story about an entrepreneur who failed multiple times before finally building a successful business. You could conclude with:

"Success isn't about avoiding failure—it's about learning from it. Every setback is just another step forward if you choose to see it that way."

This leaves the reader with a **strong, memorable lesson** that ties back to the story they just read.

2. Use a Structured List

If your chapter lends itself to multiple takeaways,

consider presenting them as a **list**. Studies suggest that people remember information better when it's grouped into odd numbers, such as three or five key points.

Example:
After telling a story about someone negotiating a raise at work, you might end with: "Here are three proven ways to increase your chances of getting a raise at work:

Prove Your Value – Track your achievements and be ready to show how your work has positively impacted the company.

Time It Right – Ask for a raise when the company is doing well financially and after you've completed a big win.

Be Ready to Walk Away – If you don't get the raise, be prepared to discuss alternative benefits or explore other opportunities."

This method is clear, actionable, and easy to remember, making it ideal for instructional or self-improvement content.

3. Weave Your Points Seamlessly into the Story
Instead of waiting until the end, you can integrate your key points throughout the narrative. This allows you

to emphasize your message naturally while you keep the story engaging.

Example:

Let's say you're writing about a marathon runner who learned the value of perseverance. Instead of saving all the lessons for the end, you can integrate them as side notes:

"By mile 15, Jake's legs felt like lead. His breath was ragged, and doubt crept in. But then he remembered what his coach had told him: 'Push through the discomfort—your body can handle more than your mind thinks it can.' So he kept going."

In this example, the lesson ("Push through the discomfort—your body can handle more than your mind thinks it can.") is naturally embedded in the story, rather than explicitly listed. This technique works well for storytelling-based writing where lessons are best shown rather than directly told.

CHOOSING THE RIGHT APPROACH

Each method has its strengths, and the best choice depends on:

✔ **The tone of your writing** – Is it more instructional, narrative-driven, or a blend of both?

✔ **Your audience** – Do they prefer clear takeaways or a more immersive experience?

✔ **The complexity of your message** – Is one strong conclusion enough, or do you need multiple points?

No matter which method you choose, the key is to ensure your reader walks away with something valuable—a lesson, an insight, or an idea that stays with them long after they've turned the page.

CLIFFHANGERS

"OH MY GOD! NOOOO!" My mother's scream jolted me from my seat.

Heart pounding, I spun around, expecting that something terrible had happened. But there she was, standing in front of the ironing board, eyes glued to the television. It was just another day, another episode of *Days of Our Lives,* and another cliffhanger that had left her in a frenzy.

Without fail, every episode would end with an unfinished sentence, a shocking twist, or a last-second revelation—something that made it impossible for her to miss tomorrow's episode. And without fail, she'd be right back in front of the TV the next day, desperate to find out what happened next.

Your book should have that same effect on your readers. Every chapter should pull them in, make them feel something, and leave them needing more.

Let's talk about how to do it.

TIPS FOR CRAFTING COMPELLING CLIFFHANGERS IN NONFICTION

End with an Unanswered Question

Pose a thought-provoking question that naturally leads into the next chapter. Example: *But what if everything you thought you knew about success was wrong?*

Leave a Story Unresolved

If you're telling a personal story, pause at a crucial moment before revealing the outcome. Example: *I had one hour to make the decision that would change my life forever...*

Introduce a Shocking Fact or Statistic

Drop a surprising piece of information right at the end of a chapter to make readers hungry for more. Example: *Studies show that 80% of people fail at this—but the 20% who don't all have one thing in common.*

Hint at What's Coming

Tease the next chapter by giving readers a sneak peek of what they're about to discover. Example: *In the next chapter, you'll learn the secret that took me from rock bottom to running a six-figure business.*

Use a Dramatic Statement

End with a powerful, declarative sentence that leaves an impact. Example: *That was the day I realized: everything had to change.*

Create Emotional Tension

Whether it's suspense, excitement, or curiosity, tap into the reader's emotions so they *need to keep reading. Ex-*

ample: I never expected what happened next. And neither will you.

By incorporating cliffhangers, you can turn your nonfiction book into a page-turner—one that keeps readers engaged, entertained, and eager to absorb every word.

THE FUNDAMENTALS OF FICTION WRITING

Here's a list of fundamental definitions every fiction writer should know:

CORE STORY ELEMENTS

•**Protagonist** – The main character of a story, typically the one the audience follows and roots for.

•**Antagonist** – The character, force, or situation that opposes the protagonist, creating conflict.

•**Plot** – The sequence of events that make up a story, typically structured around conflict and resolution.

•**Conflict** – The central struggle in a story, which can be internal (within a character) or external (against an outside force).

•**Theme** – The underlying message or idea that a story explores, such as love, power, or redemption.

STORY STRUCTURE & DEVELOPMENT

•**Exposition** – The introduction of the story, where characters, setting, and initial conflict are established.

•**Rising Action** – A series of events that build tension and develop the story's conflict.

•**Climax** – The most intense, dramatic, or significant moment of the story where the main conflict reaches a peak.

•**Falling Action** – The events following the climax that lead toward resolution.

•**Resolution (Denouement)** – The conclusion of the story where conflicts are resolved and loose ends are tied up.

CHARACTER DEVELOPMENT

•**Character Arc** – The transformation or growth of a character over the course of the story.

•**Foil** – A character who contrasts with another character, often to highlight specific traits.

•**Flat Character** – A character with little depth or development, often serving a single purpose in the story.

•**Round Character** – A complex, well-developed character with multiple facets to their personality.

•**Static Character** – A character who remains unchanged throughout the story.

•**Dynamic Character** – A character who undergoes significant change or growth.

NARRATIVE & LITERARY DEVICES

•**Point of View (POV)** – The perspective from which the story is told (first-person, third-person limited, third-person omniscient, etc.).

•**Foreshadowing** – Hints or clues about events that will occur later in the story.

•**Flashback** – A scene that takes the story back in time to reveal important background information.

•**Symbolism** – The use of objects, characters, or events to represent larger ideas.

•**Metaphor & Simile** – Comparisons used to create vivid imagery (metaphor: direct, simile: uses "like" or "as").

Genres & Subgenres

•**Fiction** – Literature created from the imagination rather than fact.

•**Fantasy** – Fiction involving magical or supernatural elements.

•**Science Fiction (Sci-Fi)** – Fiction that explores futuristic or technological themes.

•**Mystery** – Fiction centered around solving a crime or unraveling a puzzle.

•**Thriller** – A suspenseful story designed to excite and keep the reader on edge.

•**Romance** – Fiction that focuses on love and relationships.

FRAMEWORK FOR FICTION WRITING

THE HERO'S JOURNEY

Preface: I am not a fiction writer. However, the greatest storytellers and movie makers use the framework I'm about to provide to you. If you're serious about writing fiction, you should purchase and study these books: The Hero with a Thousand Faces by Joseph Campbell, The Writer's Journey by Christopher Vogler, and The Hero's 2 Journeys by Michael Hauge and Christopher Vogler.

While the details of any particular fictional story may change, the structure often remains the same. The Hero's Journey, as first mapped by Joseph Campbell in *The Hero with a Thousand Faces,* is a framework that captures this timeless pattern.

At the heart of every great story is a character who embarks on a journey—sometimes willingly, sometimes reluctantly. This journey is not just about physical travel or battles fought; it is an internal transformation, a confrontation with fear, and ultimately, a return home with newfound wisdom. This cycle, found in everything from ancient myths to blockbuster films, is the blueprint upon which many legendary stories are built.

1. The Ordinary World

Our hero's tale begins in the **Ordinary World**, the space where they are comfortable, where life follows a

If you don't have the skill or desire, there are others who can do it for you.

predictable rhythm. Think of Neo in The Matrix, trapped in the monotony of his office job, feeling that something is missing. Or Sam in Sleepless in Seattle, a grieving widower struggling to move on while raising his son. This opening moment grounds the audience in the world of the protagonist, allowing them to understand what is at stake.

2. Call to Adventure

Then comes the **Call to Adventure**—an invitation to step beyond the known world into something far greater. Sometimes it arrives as a whisper, other times as a violent shove. A distress signal, a prophecy, a mysterious letter—something disrupts the hero's status quo. Neo is contacted by Trinity, offering him the truth about reality. Sam's son calls into a radio show, setting in motion events that will challenge his grief and push him toward love again. The universe beckons, but not all heroes answer immediately.

3. The Refusal of the Call

The Refusal of the Call is a common and very human response. After all, change is frightening. The hero doubts their abilities, fears failure, or simply wishes to stay in the comfort of the familiar. Neo initially refuses to trust Morpheus, clinging to the safety of the world he knows. Sam resists dating again, believing he can never love anyone the way he loved his late wife. This hesitation makes the journey more relatable—who among us hasn't felt unprepared for life's major changes?

4. The Mentor

But help arrives. A Mentor steps in, offering guidance, wisdom, or even a revelation to aid the hero. Morpheus for Neo. Sam's son Jonah, with his unwavering belief in love, serves as the guiding force that nudges Sam forward. This figure, often embodying experience and insight, helps the hero see beyond their doubts, preparing them for the trials ahead. Sometimes, this mentor is lost along the way, forcing the hero to stand on their own (like when Morpheus was arrested by the agents leading Neo into the Matrix).

5. Crosses the Threshold

When the hero finally Crosses the Threshold, there is no turning back. They step into the unknown, leaving behind the safety of home. Whether it's Neo taking the red pill or Sam agreeing to a date, this marks the true beginning of the adventure. From here on, danger, wonder, and transformation await.

6. Tests, Allies, and Enemies

The hero soon encounters Tests, Allies, and Enemies—a series of obstacles that shape their journey. They may find loyal companions, like Trinity for Neo, or face powerful adversaries, like Agent Smith. Sam, too, is met with both allies and obstacles—his son, who pushes him toward love, and Annie's practical-minded fiancée, who represents the safe but unfulfilling path. Along the way, the hero begins to change, learn new skills, face their fears, and discover strengths they never knew they had.

7. Inmost Cave

As the journey progresses, the hero approaches a pivotal moment: the Inmost Cave. This can be a literal place—a dark fortress, a villain's lair—or an internal struggle, a realization that shakes the hero to their core. This is the moment before the storm, the deep breath before the final battle. The tension is high; failure feels imminent. Morpheus is captured by the agents and Neo must make the ultimate decision to go back into the Matrix and save him.

8. The Ordeal

Then comes the Ordeal, the most intense challenge the hero has faced. It is a moment of crisis, a life-or-death struggle where everything hangs in the balance. Neo must fight Agent Smith and embrace his destiny as The One. Sam, after nearly missing his chance, must confront his fear of letting go and open his heart again. This trial is what separates the old self from the new, forging the hero in fire.

9. The Reward

If the hero survives, they emerge changed. They claim their Reward—sometimes a physical object, like a sword or treasure, but more often, a realization of inner strength. The hero is not the same as when they began. Yet, the journey is not over. They must still return home, often facing:

10. The Road Back

The Road Back, a final series of tests that push them to their limits once more.

11. The Resurrection

The Resurrection is the climax, where the hero faces their ultimate challenge, proving that they have truly changed. This is the moment of rebirth, where the hero overcomes their greatest fear or sacrifice. In The Matrix, Neo dies and is reborn, now fully realizing his power. In Sleepless in Seattle, Sam, despite all his doubts, takes a leap of faith and meets Annie atop the Empire State Building, embracing the possibility of love once more.

12. Returns with the Elixir

At last, the hero Returns with the Elixir, bringing back newfound wisdom, power, or change to their world. This could be literal—Neo freeing others from the Matrix—or symbolic, like Sam rediscovering love and hope, no longer held back by grief. The journey is complete, the world has been altered, and the hero has fulfilled their purpose.

Whether set in a dystopian future or in the modern world of romance, this framework provides writers with a roadmap to create compelling, meaningful stories. Not every tale must follow it exactly, but understanding its core elements helps craft narratives that resonate.

Where is your hero now? Where are they going? And what will they bring back when they return? Every journey, no matter how grand or small, has the power to change not just the hero, but the world around them.

Timothy O. Bond

Congratulations!

You've made it to the end of this journey, and by now, you should feel equipped with the knowledge and tools to bring your book to life. Writing a manuscript is no small feat, but with the right mindset, structure, and strategies, it becomes a rewarding and achievable goal.

Throughout this book, we've explored the essential components of manuscript writing—starting with overcoming fear, understanding the anatomy of a manuscript, and learning how to structure your work. We've looked at the art of storytelling, where facts tell but stories sell; we've taken the hero's journey; and we've covered the importance of showing, not telling, to engage your readers.

We've also taken a closer look at the practical side of writing, from creating a schedule to organizing your thoughts in a structured framework. Each chapter builds upon the last, providing you with a clear roadmap to follow from the initial idea all the way to the final draft.

But remember, writing is not a race. It's a process, and it's okay to move at your own pace. There will be days of inspiration, and there will be days of frustration, but each word you write brings you one step closer to achieving your goal.

As you embark on your writing journey, always keep in mind that you are a creator. The world is waiting for the story only you can tell. Embrace the process, trust in your voice, and don't be afraid to share your unique perspective with the world.

Now, take a deep breath. It's time to start writing. The world needs your book. So, let's get to it.

Ready to Take Your Manuscript to the Next Level?

If you're looking for personalized, one-on-one support to bring your book to life, our Manuscript Coaching and Co-Writing Service is exactly what you need. With direct access to a professional writing coach, you'll receive expert guidance on every line of your manuscript. From polishing your prose to perfecting your message, we'll work together to ensure your book is crafted to its highest potential.

Our coaching isn't just about feedback—it's about transformation. You'll receive real-time coaching, in-depth editing, and the motivation you need to move forward with confidence. Our clients don't just finish their books; they finish them faster and with the peace of mind that their manuscript is ready to make a lasting impact.

This is your chance to work alongside a dedicated expert who will help you turn your vision into a book that truly changes lives. Don't miss out—your story deserves to be heard, and we're here to make sure it gets out there in the most powerful way possible.

Contact: Timothy Bond
615-585-0143
TrueVinePublishing.org
TrueVinePublishing@gmail.com

www.ingramcontent.com/pod-product-compliance
Lightning Source LLC
Chambersburg PA
CBHW051221120626
46547CB00013B/1451